WILDLI

G000145597

Steve Parish Publishing Pty Ltd

The dingo is Australia's wild dog

WILDLIFE

Australia's wildlife consists of much, much more than the majestic, leaping red kangaroo and the cute, climbing koala, though those animals represent the continent's remarkable marsupials.

Australia has more than 750 species of birds, including splendid parrots, spectacular waterbirds and majestic birds of prey, and the land abounds in snakes, lizards and other reptiles, including the awesome saltwater crocodile. Frogs live in even the most sun-blasted deserts, and are in their element in the cool dampness of the rainforests.

The seas around Australia's coasts provide multiple habitats for animals of all sorts, from the tiny coral polyps which built the fabulous Great Barrier Reef to the mighty whales which yearly make their epic journeys along the coastlines.

The years I have spent watching Australia's wild creatures have been rich and rewarding. This small book presents a few of my favourite portraits for your pleasure.

• Common wombat •

It is a pity wombats do not spend more daylight time in the open, for they are delightful animals, intelligent and full of personality. However, while the sun shines they are usually curled up asleep underground in their burrows. They emerge to feed at night (left) or, occasionally, on overcast, dull days (opposite).

◆ Koala ◆

The koala above looks alert as it reaches for a pawful of gum leaves to eat, but the low energy content of its diet ensures it sleeps for around 20 hours out of every 24.

• Cockatoos and parrots •

The sulphur-crested cockatoo (above) is a splendid squawker. The smaller crimson rosella (opposite) has a much more melodious call.

Over: Australian king-parrot

• Rainforest birds •

Many rainforest birds are demurely coloured,
like the Lewin's honeyeater opposite or grey
fantail above. This camouflages them amidst
vegetation, while their calls identify them
and claim their breeding territories.

• Wallabies and kangaroos •

A wallaby is simply a small kangaroo. The Bennett's wallaby, shown with its pouch young, or joey, at left, and the grey kangaroo, opposite, both rely on long hopping bounds to escape danger. The young of these animals are born undeveloped, blind and naked, and spend their first few months safe in their mother's warm pouch.

Female common wallaroo

Male red kangaroo

• Possums •

Many possums live in trees, and have grasping hands and feet and long, flexible tails. They are active at night, and regard the world through large, forward-gazing eyes. The green ringtail possum opposite is a rainforest species. The eastern pygmy possum at right is feeding on nectar.

• Gliding possums •

Sugar gliders belong to a group of possums with membranes between fore legs and hind legs which enable them to swoop from one tree to another. They spend daytime curled in a nest in a hollow limb and at night feed on nectar, insects and tree sap.

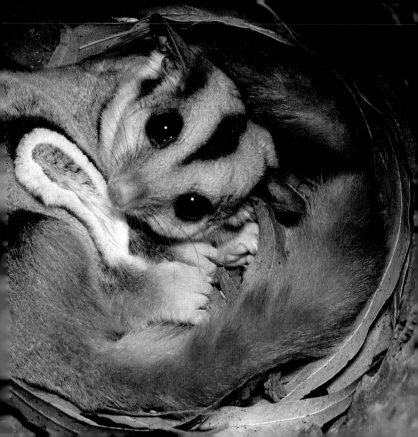

◆ Waterbirds ◆

Water is a precious resource over
most of Australia and waterbirds
may have to travel long distances
from one swamp or billabong to
another. The plumed whistling-
duck (above) and Australian pelican
(opposite) are both excellent flyers.

◆ Frogs ◆

When rain falls across northern Australia, the thoughts of frogs turn to producing a new generation. The pale frogs above are mating, while the male dainty green tree-frog opposite is calling for a female.

Over: Green tree-frog

• Tasmanian devil •

The inquisitive air of the
Tasmanian devil portrayed at
right is probably more typical
of this dog-sized marsupial
than the gaping jaws opposite.
Such a fierce expression is
usually an attempt to
intimidate a fellow devil and
filch a few mouthfuls of tasty
road-kill or other easily
obtained meal.

• Short-beaked echidna •

The echidna waddles around the bushland, digging up ants and termites and eating them with its long, sticky tongue. Faced by danger, it scrabbles frantically at the ground beneath it and rapidly sinks downwards, protected by its bristling spines.

• Flying-foxes are megabats •

Flying-foxes are large bats which eat fruit and nectar. During daytime, they hang around in groups, but at night they unfurl large membranous wings and flap off to find food. They are sociable, intelligent animals, which can live only in warmer areas where fruits are constantly available. A grey-headed flying-fox is shown opposite; a spectacled flying-fox is shown at right.

◆ Lizards ◆

Two of Australia's most spectacular large lizards belong to
the group called the dragons.
They are the beautifully-
camouflaged southern forest
dragon (left), a rainforest
species, and the gloriously-
caped frilled lizard (opposite),
which raises colourful folds of
skin around its neck in
defence and to rid its body of
excess heat.

• Snakes with all-purpose tongues •

Non-venomous snakes such as the green python
(opposite) and diamond python (above) crush
prey in coils of their muscular bodies. They feel,
taste and smell things with their tongues.

• Emus •

These large, flightless birds are widespread
on mainland Australia. Emus eat grass, herbs
and some insects. After the female lays the
eggs, the male incubates them and then looks
after the chicks for the next 18 months.

◆ Tropical butterflies ◆

Australia's tropical rainforests
are home to the magnificent
Cairns birdwing butterfly
(opposite) and ulysses
butterfly (right). Like all
butterflies, these gorgeous
insects spend some time as
caterpillars, feeding hungrily
on plants peculiar to the
species. Destroy the plants
on which they feed and the
butterflies will disappear also.

• Greater bilby •

Who would look at a European rabbit when they could contemplate one of these exquisite creatures, with its silken fur and delicate, quivering nose. There were once two sorts of bilby living in burrows in Australia's Outback. Now the lesser bilby has been exterminated by land clearing, stock grazing, feral cats, foxes and rabbits – it is to be hoped that the greater bilby shown here will survive.

✦ Birds of prey ✦

Australia's birds of prey have hooked beaks and sharp-taloned feet. The two species shown here live near water. The osprey (above) feeds exclusively on fish. The white-bellied sea-eagle (opposite) is an opportunist, capable of taking large prey if it is hungry enough.

• Platypus •

With its dense fur and eyes and nostrils on top of its head, the platypus is adapted to dive for food. The feet are webbed, though the webbing can be turned under, as shown here, when it travels on land or digs into a river bank to make a resting or nesting burrow. A baby platypus hatches from an egg, then is fed on milk produced by special glands on its mother's belly.

⬩ Dingo ⬩

"Yellow-dog-dingo" (which may be black, or ginger, or white) is part of Australian legend, and many people are surprised when told there is no evidence of dingos existing on the continent before around 3500 years ago. They are closely related to a species living in South-east Asia, and probably came to Australia with seafarers around that time.

⋆ Laughing kookaburra ⋆

This giant kingfisher lives in
family groups, which greet the
dawn with a chorus of laughing,
chuckling calls.

• Little Penguin •

This is the only penguin to nest in Australia, visiting southern shores to excavate nests in sand dunes or under boulders. Both parents incubate the eggs, then travel to sea each dawn to gather fish to feed their fluffy chicks. At dusk, they leap from the surf and waddle up the beach, crops bulging with goodies for their offspring, performing the well-known penguin parades.

• Saltwater crocodile •

This northern coastal reptile is an aquatic predator whose basic design is so effective it has remained unchanged for over two hundred million years. The fearsome teeth are constantly replaced. They interlock, so that prey is gripped as if in a vice studded with nails. The jaws close with such force that even if the victim escapes, the impact has killed the tissue around the wounds and it later sloughs away.

Lionfish live on coral reefs. Their gorgeous fins are tipped with venomous barbs.

This pink anemonefish lives safely within the stinging tentacles of a sea anemone.

♦ Australian sea-lions ♦

There are only between 3500 and 5000
of these sea-going, fish-eating marine
mammals. These live on Kangaroo
Island, off the coast of South Australia.

◆ Whales and dolphins ◆

Humpback whales and bottlenose
dolphins come to many places on
Australian coasts where they may be
watched by – and sometimes watch –
humans.

Steve Parish has recorded Australia, its wildlife and its people with his camera for many years. Steve's aim is to show people the marvels that exist in this long-isolated continent, with its unique cities, landscapes, plants and animals. His passion for Australia, and his awareness that urgent human action is needed to preserve its wildlife and places of beauty lends intensity to his superb photographs and evocative writing. Steve and his wife and partner Jan founded Steve Parish Publishing Pty Ltd to share with the world their vision of Australia.

Steve Parish
PUBLISHING

Photos: pp. 23, 23 Belinda Wright; pp. 48, 49 Peter Marsack
(Lochman Transparencies); p. 62 Mark Simmons

Text: Pat Slater

PRINTED IN AUSTRALIA
ISBN 1 875932 66 6